MTLE Physical Education (Grades K–12) Exam

"You never fail until you stop trying" - Albert Einstein

For inquiries;
info@xmprep.com

Unauthorised copying of any part of this test is illegal.

MTLE Physical Education (Grades K–12) Exam #1

Test Taking Tips

☐ Take a deep breath and relax

☐ Read directions carefully

☐ Read the questions thoroughly

☐ Make sure you understand what is being asked

☐ Go over all of the choices before you answer

☐ Paraphrase the question

☐ Eliminate the options you know are wrong

☐ Check your work

☐ Think positively and do your best

Table of Contents

SECTION 1	
DIRECTION	1
PRACTICE TEST	2 - 16
ANSWER KEY	17
SECTION 2	
DIRECTION	18
PRACTICE TEST	19 - 30
ANSWER KEY	31
SECTION 3	
DIRECTION	32
PRACTICE TEST	33 - 44
ANSWER KEY	45
SECTION 4	
DIRECTION	46
PRACTICE TEST	47 - 61
ANSWER KEY	62
SECTION 5	
DIRECTION	63
PRACTICE TEST	64 - 73
ANSWER KEY	74

Copyright © Educational Testing Group, All rights reserved.
This booklet may not be reproduced and transmitted in any form by any means without the permission of the publisher.
This booklet has been prepared and printed in USA.

TEST DIRECTION

DIRECTIONS

Read the questions carefully and then choose the ONE best answer to each question.

Be sure to allocate your time carefully so you are able to complete the entire test within the testing session. You may go back and review your answers at any time.

You may use any available space in your test booklet for scratch work.

Questions in this booklet are not actual test questions but they are the samples for commonly asked questions.

This test aims to cover all topics which may appear on the actual test. However some topics may not be covered.

Studying this booklet will be preparing you for the actual test. It will not guarantee improving your test score but it will help you pass your exam on the first attempt.

Some useful tips for answering multiple choice questions;

- Start with the questions that you can easily answer.

- Underline the keywords in the question.

- Be sure to read all the choices given.

- Watch for keywords such as NOT, always, only, all, never, completely.

- Do not forget to answer every question.

1

1

In which of the following domains of learning do learning about rules, traditions, history, and etiquette of sports belong?

A) Cognitive
B) Psychomotor
C) Associative
D) Affective

2

Which of the following domains of learning do learning about sports rules, traditions, history, and etiquette fall?

A) Interactions
B) Mental skills under cognitive
C) Physical skills under psychomotor
D) Emotional skills under affective

3

Which of the following sports enhances cooperation, honesty, and trust within and between teams because it relies on the players to call their own infractions and to try to play within the rules of the game?

A) Ultimate
B) Rugby
C) Football
D) Squash

4

Which of the following part of the brain is responsible for refining skilled movements?

A) Cerebellum
B) Pons
C) Cerebrum
D) Medulla oblongata

5

What kind of activity primarily describes organized sports according to most sports sociologists?

A) Player friendly
B) Institutionalized
C) Family sports
D) Mind games

6

Which of the following represents angular motion?

A) The knees of a cyclist
B) The legs of a runner
C) The arms of a swimmer
D) All of the above

7

The British tradition of fair play is a fair treatment of people without cheating or being dishonest.

Which of the following is the goal of educators to students in using the British tradition of fair play in physical education programs?

A) Sportsmanship
B) Self-assessment
C) Self-confidence
D) Teamwork

8

Locomotor is defined as the act or power of moving from place to place. In which of the following locomotor skills, each foot have two tasks to complete before the weight is transferred to the other foot?

A) Skipping
B) Walking
C) Running
D) Galloping

9

Which of the following does a soccer player exhibits when he decided to kick the ball in an open space or the area wherein none of his opponents is present?

A) Management
B) Mastery
C) Strategy
D) Exhibition

10

Which of the following is the best fitness test to be used by a physical education teacher in assessing the fitness of students with disabilities?

A) President's Challenge
B) Brockport Physical Fitness Test
C) ActivityGram
D) Fitnessgram

11

Which of the following factors affects the speed of an object thrown overhand?

A) Grip-release
B) Wrist Flexion
C) Hip rotation
D) Hand-held proximity

12

What should be the best range of maximum heart rate in terms of percentage in characterizing the student's exercise for health-related fitness in physical education class?

A) 85-100%
B) 60-85%
C) 40-60%
D) 20-40%

13

The Internet is a global computer network providing a variety of information and communication facilities, consisting of interconnected networks using standardized communication protocols.

Which of the following is the advantage of the Internet in doing research for physical education students?

A) Finding sources of fitness equipment and materials
B) Creating a list of physical activities used throughout the world
C) Comparing the advantages and disadvantages of various physical fitness regimens
D) Locating appropriate resources for individual physical activities and nutritional needs and guidelines

CONTINUE ▶

14

Cooling down is an easy exercise, done after a more intense activity, to allow the body to gradually transition to a resting or near-resting state while stretching is a form of physical exercise in which a specific muscle or tendon is deliberately flexed.

Which of the following is the benefit of doing cool-down and stretching activities after strenuous cardiorespiratory fitness activities?

A) Prevent an abrupt decrease in the glucose level
B) Prevent the reduction of carbohydrates and fat composition in the body
C) Prevent muscle soreness and blood pooling in the extremities
D) Trigger a final surge in metabolic rate before the body reverts to a resting state

15

Why does the warm-up period before exercise help in preserving the joints?

A) Because it increases the proportion of blood in the thoracic cavity.
B) Becuase it stimulates the release of synovial fluid, which lubricates the joints.
C) Because it activates the sympathetic nervous system.
D) Because it encourages the uptake of lactic acid.

16

Which of the following should a teacher initially provide in teaching a closed skill?

A) A changing environment with varying rates of skill performance
B) A changing environment with a constant rate of skill performance
C) A stable environment with varying rates of skill performance
D) A stable environment with a stable rate of skill performance

17

In order to learn a new takedown technique, which of the following technology applications would best support a wrestler?

A) Gathering information from co-wrestlers
B) Proper execution of viewed pictures on a video screen
C) Reading about the proper technique and procedure on the internet
D) Watching other wrestler's performance

18

On athlete's sports performance, a primary short-term effect of amphetamines is illustrated by which of the following?

A) The risk of injury decreases
B) Feelings of alertness increases
C) Thinking process decreases
D) The growth of muscles increases

19

Which of the following improvements is experienced by people who do yoga according to the Mayo Clinic?

A) Production of testosterone, clearer eyesight, and younger looks
B) Healthier skin, digestive health, and more active
C) Becoming more fit, management of chronic conditions, and reduce stress
D) Faster thinking, increase in appetite, and clearer eyesight

20

Total daily calorie needs are the number of calories need to maintain per day.

Which of the following stages of growth and development is the highest amount of total daily calorie needs?

A) Late adulthood
B) Early adulthood
C) Infancy
D) Adolescence

21

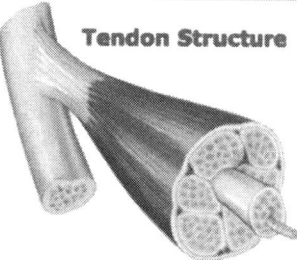

Tendon Structure

Tendon is a flexible but inelastic cord of strong fibrous collagen tissue. Which of the following is the main function of tendons in the skeletal system?

A) Attach bones to muscles
B) Attach bones to other bones
C) Attach ligaments to muscle fibers
D) Act as the source of calcium phosphate

22

Rico's daily intake, as well as his daily expenditure of calories, is 3,000. Judith has 3,000 daily intakes of calories while she has a daily expenditure of calories of 2,000. Timothy has a calorie daily intake of 2,000 and a daily expenditure of 2,800 calories. Lastly, Aliana has a daily intake of 1,000 calories and a daily expenditure of 4,000 calories.

Who among the four persons would most likely to lose weight safely?

A) Aliana
B) Timothy
C) Judith
D) Rico

23

A kick is a physical strike using the leg: foot, heel, tibia, thigh or knee.

Which of the following would help students who fail to step forward with their kicking foot and leap onto their non-kicking foot just before the kick?

A) Set concentration on one pattern to generate controlled kick.
B) Place two poly spots at the desired distances in front of each student and instruct students to step on one and leap onto the other before contacting the ball.
C) Make a mark for every step, leap, and kick off the student to monitor their kick positions.
D) Place a plastic cone in front of each student's dominant side and instruct students to step, leap, and kick without a ball, trying to skim the cone.

24

Dance is a performing art form consisting of purposefully selected sequences of human movement.

Which of the following styles of dance will be most appropriate to introduce to students that have mastery of fundamental skills for rhythmic movement?

A) Line dance
B) Contemporary dance
C) Modern dance
D) Ballroom dance

25

In order to assess the skills of students during a basketball skills unit, which of the following would be the most appropriate way a teacher do?

A) Have them watch basketball games
B) Have them make an essay about basketball
C) Match two teams and watch which team will win
D) When moving through the unit, assess learners by developing a rubric

26

In order for a physical education teacher to complete and adhere to at the beginning of the school year in an effort to establish good classroom management, which of the following sets of tasks would be the best?

A) Learning the basics of an activity
B) Make posters for announcements
C) Letting the students do fitness tests whenever they want
D) Having an organized system of rules, records, lesson with the participation of students

27

A mother wants to determine what her 10-year-old child needs for bone growth and development.

Which of the following nutritional areas should be focused?

A) Adequate potassium intake
B) Adequate B-vitamins intake
C) Adequate fiber intake
D) Adequate calcium intake

28

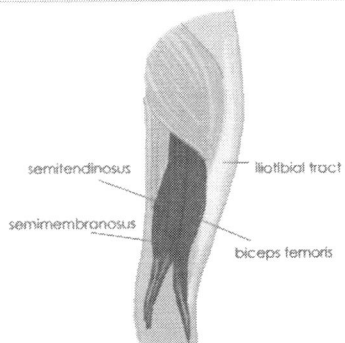

The hamstring muscle group consists of three separate muscles; the semitendinosus, semimembranosus and biceps femoris. They originate from the lower part of the pelvis and insert into the back of the shin bone. When contracting they mainly bend the knee and extend the hip joint.

One of your students has been strained in his hamstring muscle. Which of the following pieces would be the proper treatment?

A) Applying ice and compressing the leg
B) Applying ice and stretching the leg
C) Applying heat and compressing the leg
D) Applying heat and stretching the leg

29

Locomotor skills are the basic ways to move, the building blocks of coordination.

Which of the following locomotor skills for a five-year-old would be most difficult?

A) Galloping for a bed length distance
B) Hopping on one foot from one end of a classroom to the other end
C) Climbing up and down stairs without using the handrail
D) Jumping over low objects

30.

A hazard is any agent that can cause harm or damage to life, health, property or the environment. In ensuring physical education facility to be free of hazards, which of the following is the most important procedure?

A) Ask students to use the facilities with care and not so often in order to avoid defects.
B) Attend seminars and conferences that involve specific case safety issues in different schools.
C) Make sure that safety inspections occur regularly and that resulting concerns are quickly addressed.
D) Compare physical education safety procedures to occupational safety standards and matching procedures to industry standards.

31.

Diabetes is a group of metabolic disorders in which there are high blood sugar levels over a prolonged period.

Which of the following is the benefit of exercise on treatment plans of diabetic people?

A) Reduce the build-up of glucose in the blood
B) Prevent diabetes-induced changes in vision
C) Increase the production of insulin in the pancreas
D) Reduce body weight of diabetic people

32

The forehand in tennis is a shot made by swinging the racket across one's body with the hand moving palm-first. On the other hand, backhand is a stroke played with the back of the hand facing in the direction of the stroke, typically starting with the arm crossing the body.

In order to allow a player to contact the ball in front of the body, there must be a pivot on the back foot and a step toward the net. Which of the following is the most appropriate technique?

A) Keeping back straight while bending knees
B) Making sure that the rotation of racquet is counterclockwise
C) Pointing the top of the racquet towards the opponent
D) Turning the shoulders early in preparation for the swing

33

In secondary physical education programs, which of the following is a major challenge?

A) Providing adequate time and activities to encourage students to adopt a lasting ethic of physical activity
B) Providing activities that can be differentiated from middle school programs
C) Providing activities that would promote active and healthy lifestyle
D) Providing activities that each student can enjoy and appreciate

34

Which of the following should be emphasized to children to have healthy eating practices and patterns?

A) Stimulate growth hormone production faster
B) Increase endurance and stamina without exercise
C) Reduce time for sleep to have more play time
D) Help prevent both short- and long-term health problems such as colds, dental cavities, and obesity

35

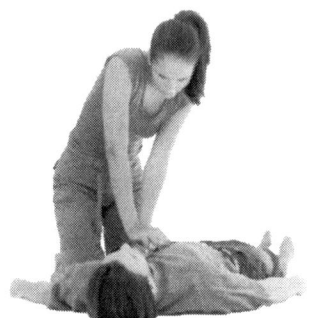

Cardiopulmonary resuscitation or CPR is an emergency technique used on someone whose heart or breathing has stopped. This is commonly used in emergency situations like a heart attack or near drowning. In the following sequence of procedure in doing the protocol of CPR, which choice has the correct sequence?

1. Open airway

2. Check to breathe

3. Supply two full breaths

4. Check pulse

A) 4 – 3 – 2
B) 4 – 1 – 3
C) 3 – 4 – 1
D) 1 – 3 – 4

36

Which of the following is the advantage of incorporating wellness technology programs in schools' physical education program?

A) Provide students and teachers with immediate access to data and allowing students to design, monitor and progress toward personal wellness goals.
B) Reduce time in manually demonstrating physical education lessons.
C) Establish a networking system by which physical education teachers can easily communicate with stu-dents' families, faculty, and service providers.
D) Allow students to evaluate their wellness and give information to their families in achieving better goals of awareness.

37

Why is Society of Health and Physical Educators (SHAPE America) considered an important resource for beginning physical educators?

A) Because it disseminates current information in order to enhance the knowledge about physical education and improve practice
B) Because it allows access to a blog that allows parents, students, and teachers to cooperate with each other
C) Because it provides liability insurance for physical educations once a problem comes up
D) Because its website contains all the necessary lesson plans that can be used by a physical education teacher

38

Standing toe touch is bending at the waist, keeping your legs straight until you can relax and let your upper body hang down in front of you. Let your arms and hands hang down naturally.

Which of the following is the main reason that a straight-legged standing toe-touch is a high-risk exercise?

A) Maximizes hamstring stretch reflex
B) Elongates cervical ligaments causing muscle sore
C) Increases pressure on lumbar disks and overstretch lumbar ligaments
D) Uses the latissimus dorsi as a shoulder extensor, which hyper-extends the shoulders.

39

The narration is the act of telling a story, usually in some kind of chronological order. A dance teacher lets his students watch a dance performance with narration that explains the story of the dance being performed before doing their routines.

Which of the following is the benefit of narration on the students' understanding of dance?

A) Examples of giving facial expressions
B) Developing an emotional connection with other dancers
C) Showing movement can convey meaning
D) Showing artistic and aesthetic expression

School management is looking for strategies that would promote the values of their physical education programs.

Which of the following would be the most practical and effective method?

A) Use a variety of media and opportunities to communicate with students, families, and school community members about fitness and recreational resources and activities and their benefits.

B) Give flyers with instruction to teachers and students that they also need to be sent out to the community.

C) Create more routines that emphasize motor learning in students.

D) Assist teachers and administrators in locating and accessing inexpensive fitness and recreational resources and facilities in the community.

SECTION 1

#	Answer	Topic	Subtopic	#	Answer	Topic	Subtopic	#	Answer	Topic	Subtopic	#	Answer	Topic	Subtopic
1	A	TB	SB1	11	C	TB	SB3	21	A	TA	SA1	31	A	TA	SA2
2	B	TA	SA1	12	B	TA	SA1	22	B	TA	SA2	32	D	TB	SB3
3	A	TB	SB2	13	D	TB	SB1	23	B	TB	SB1	33	A	TB	SB1
4	A	TB	SB2	14	C	TA	SA2	24	A	TB	SB2	34	D	TA	SA2
5	B	TB	SB1	15	B	TA	SA1	25	D	TA	SA2	35	D	TB	SB3
6	D	TB	SB3	16	D	TB	SB1	26	D	TA	SA2	36	A	TB	SB1
7	A	TB	SB2	17	B	TA	SA2	27	D	TA	SA1	37	A	TB	SB1
8	A	TB	SB3	18	B	TA	SA1	28	A	TA	SA2	38	C	TA	SA2
9	C	TB	SB3	19	C	TA	SA1	29	B	TB	SB2	39	C	TB	SB1
10	B	TB	SB1	20	D	TA	SA2	30	C	TB	SB1	40	A	TB	SB1

Topics & Subtopics

Code	Description
SA1	Health Knowledge
SA2	Health Instruction
SB1	Planning Instruction
SB2	Student Growth & Development

Code	Description
SB3	Planning Activities
TA	Health Education
TB	Physical Education

TEST DIRECTION

DIRECTIONS

Read the questions carefully and then choose the ONE best answer to each question.

Be sure to allocate your time carefully so you are able to complete the entire test within the testing session. You may go back and review your answers at any time.

You may use any available space in your test booklet for scratch work.

Questions in this booklet are not actual test questions but they are the samples for commonly asked questions.

This test aims to cover all topics which may appear on the actual test. However some topics may not be covered.

Studying this booklet will be preparing you for the actual test. It will not guarantee improving your test score but it will help you pass your exam on the first attempt.

Some useful tips for answering multiple choice questions;

- Start with the questions that you can easily answer.

- Underline the keywords in the question.

- Be sure to read all the choices given.

- Watch for keywords such as NOT, always, only, all, never, completely.

- Do not forget to answer every question.

1

Which of the following devices is worn by a walker or runner for recording the number of steps taken, thereby showing approximately the distance traveled?

A) Tanita
B) Pedometer
C) Spirometer
D) Bioelectrical impedance analyzer

2

What factor is developed when a person is swimming ½ mile four times a week?

A) Agility
B) Flexibility
C) Balance
D) Aerobic Fitness

3

Which of the following practice alternatives would best promote motor learning and safety for potentially dangerous sports like downhill skiing and pole vaulting?

A) Distributed
B) Progressive-part
C) Part
D) Whole

4

Motor learning and safety for potentially injurious sports were best promoted by which of the following practice alternatives?

A) Distributed part
B) Whole part
C) Progressive part
D) Partial part

5

The direct measurement of the rate of oxygen consumption during exercise is primarily determined by which of the following parameter?

A) VO2 max
B) Pulse rate
C) Minute ventilation
D) Red blood cell count

6

Which of the following is reduced by following the correct racing posture of a swimmer, a cyclist or a downhill skier?

A) Speed
B) Gravitational force
C) Turbulence
D) Risk of injury

CONTINUE ▶

7

What instrument can be used to determine an individual's body fat composition most effectively?

A) A skinfold caliper
B) Scales and a height-weight chart
C) Hydrostatic weighing
D) Measurements of the circumference of the waist, hips, thighs, and arms of the person.

8

Kinesthesis is the ability of the person to feel movements of the limbs and body. Which of the following is the other name for kinesthesis?

A) Proprioception
B) Coordination
C) Reflex action
D) Tonic neck response

9

A code of professional conduct is a necessary component of any profession to maintain standards for the individuals within that profession to adhere. It brings about accountability, responsibility and trust to the individuals that the profession serves.

Based on professional codes of conduct for physical educators, which of the following is an unethical practice?

A) Discuss student's issues with his/her parent/guardian in helping the student.
B) Use a physical education assessment tool or test for a purpose for which it was not designed or validated.
C) Revise instruction based on informal data assessment.
D) Compile group results in suggesting improvement or need of other fitness resources.

10

Which of the following is the best choice of available fitness tests for a teacher to use to assess students with disabilities?

A) Brockport Physical Fitness Test
B) Basic Fitness test
C) Limited fitness activity
D) Fitnessgram

CONTINUE ▶

11

A strain is a stretching or tearing of muscle or tendon.

Which of the following will most likely to result in a muscle pull or strain?

A) Doing varying exercises every session
B) Interchanging work of upper and lower body every other day
C) Using static stretching rather than dynamic stretching to cool down after strength training
D) Exercising a particular muscle group without working for its opposing muscle group (e.g., quadriceps but not hamstrings)

12

The balance beam is a cube / rectangular object an artistic gymnastics apparatus, as well as the event, performed using the apparatus.

Which of the following is the main advantage of female adolescents in showing greater motor control on a balance beam than male adolescents?

A) Shorter legs and feet
B) Lighter body weight
C) Lower center of gravity
D) Greater body density relative to overall body composition

13

A modification is a change or alteration, usually to make something work better.

Which of the following modifications would increase the success rate of all soccer players?

A) Widen the goal
B) More players in the field
C) Larger field area
D) Increase team members

14

The most common problem encountered in most characteristic of the primitive stage of forward rolling is due to which of the following problems?

A) The curl is lost
B) The chin is tucked
C) Head contact by hands
D) The knees and hips are flexed

15

Which of the following best describes the effect of increasing rates of sedentary activity and poor dietary practices over rates of physical activities in adolescents?

A) Increase in stress-related disease
B) Increase in mineral-deficiency diseases
C) Increase in fatigue-related diseases
D) Increase in incidence of obesity-related diseases

16

Which of the following is not included in the list of characteristics when performing a correct mature form of striking a ball with a racquet?

A) A person is coiling and rotating the body forward as the racquet is swung
B) A person is putting weight on the back foot and then shifting to the front foot as the racquet is swung
C) A person is stopping the racquet at the point of contact with the ball
D) A person is taking a forward step with the foot opposite to the striking arm

17

What is the importance of the Society of Health and Physical Educators (SHAPE AMERICA) which serves as a resource for beginning physical educators?

A) In case of a problem, it provides insurance

B) It contains the complete curriculum a school needs

C) It enhances parent-teacher collaboration by allowing an access to a blog

D) To enhance physical education knowledge and improve practice, it disseminates current information

18

Which of the following are the two principles of modern muscle strength and endurance conditioning followed by a person who lifted a newborn bull onto his shoulders each day until the bull became fully mature?

A) Overload and progression
B) Retention and stress
C) Progression and intensity
D) Strength and variable resistance

19

Transfer of learning is the dependency of human conduct, learning, or performance on prior experience.

Which of the following conditions will most likely benefit from the principle of transfer of learning when a student is learning a new complex motor skill?

A) New motor skill is similar to one already mastered.

B) New motor skill is a discrete skill rather than a continuous one.

C) The student has no previous knowledge about the new motor skill.

D) The student has the ability to openly take comments from teachers regardless of good or bad

20

Motor Behavior is a program in exercise science that prepares students to enter physical or occupational therapy or other related professional schools.

Which of the following is being integrated into motor behaviors that is when the ability to time movements to intercept a moving object is dependent?

A) Source of the force and the object's weight

B) Air resistance and the object's weight

C) Momentum and relative positions of the object

D) Sensory information about the speed and direction of the object

21

A risk factor is something that increases your chance of getting a disease.

Which of the following modifiable risk factors are associated with coronary artery disease according to the American Heart Association?

A) Age and ethnic background
B) Stress and physical inactivity
C) Age and family history
D) Smoking and alcohol consumption

22

Carbohydrate is any of a large group of organic compounds occurring in foods and living tissues and including sugars, starch, and cellulose.

Which of the following are the two main functions of carbohydrates in the body?

A) Build and repair body tissues
B) Provide energy for cells and maintaining an energy reserve
C) Synthesize and secrete complex fatty acid substances
D) Repair damaged cells and creating new ones

23

Which of the following is the benefit of setting an activity on students that evaluate their heart rate after walking, jogging and sprinting with slow, medium or fast pace?

A) Explaining the difference between aerobic and anaerobic activities
B) Helping student to identify their normal heart rate
C) Teaching student in calculating respiration rates during aerobic activity
D) Introducing students to basic cardio-respiratory fitness principles in the context of a physical activity

24

Self-worth is the opinion you have about yourself and the value you place on yourself while self-esteem reflects a person's overall subjective emotional evaluation of his or her own worth.

A school has decided to conduct a field day with physical activities for students. One of the activities goals is to hone student's self-esteem and sense of self-worth. Which of the following would be the most appropriate organizational approach?

A) Creating more group activities than individual activities
B) Demonstrating activities that emphasize balance and speed
C) Only allow students to activities based on their capabilities
D) Offering activities that allow students of varying fitness and skill levels to achieve individual success

CONTINUE ▶

25

A basketball coach separates his team in pairs. He instructs them that one will be doing chest pass and other will make a bounce pass facing each other and switch roles at the end of the line.

Which of the following would be the main objective of the activity?

A) Practicing teamwork
B) Developing offensive footwork while passing
C) Practicing dribbling skills
D) Developing skills in passing

26

An injury is a damage to the body caused by external force.

During basketball games, which of the following situations would most likely to result in an injury?

A) A distinguishable line of the court
B) Nonfunctioning overhead middle fluorescent light
C) Narrow safety zone between an end line of the court and a gym wall
D) A facilitator table located in the center of the court which is in meter-distance of the outside line

27

Educational assessment is the systematic process of documenting and using empirical data on the knowledge, skill, attitudes, and beliefs to refine programs and improve student learning.

Which of the following should be ensured to physical education assessment strategies when doing careful planning?

A) Develop based on students' comfortability and capability
B) Align with student outcomes and instructional frameworks
C) Conjunction with teacher's standard of evaluation
D) Present in a formal written format which is familiar to students

28

During the start of the school year, which of the following lists are the best practices to be followed by a PE teacher to establish good classroom management?

A) Posting rules on the wall, not smiling and learning the names of the students.
B) Teaching students a predetermined signal to stop activity, establishing rules and reviewing them with the students, creating a record-keeping system
C) Posting rules on the wall, creating a record-keeping system and having an open gym period
D) Learning the names of the students, playing fun games with the students and teaching the class how to do warm-ups

29

Nutrition is the process of providing or obtaining the food necessary for health and growth. To promote optimum growth and development in young children, which of the following is the suggested nutritional practice?

A) Consuming high dietary fiber for good digestion
B) Consuming more protein to aid in developing more muscles
C) Consuming more fatty foods to increase stored energy
D) Consuming three moderately large meals and avoiding or limiting snacks and treats to promote desirable eating patterns

30

Physical Strength is generated through the interaction of muscles, skeleton, tendons, and ligaments and through energy conversion in the muscles. After the age of 20, both males and females achieve their maximum physical strength.

Which of the following could be accounted for this change at that age level?

A) Degradation of muscles has started to take place
B) Muscular cross-sectional areas are largest
C) A free radical formation is fastest
D) The rate of metabolism is slowest

31

Which of the following should a skills-based approach fitness education programs for middle and high school students provide?

A) A discussion on how the environment affects fitness
B) Sufficient practice opportunities in one or two movement form to develop high levels of proficiency in those areas
C) List of available places that can provide adequate resources for the fitness program they specifically need.
D) The knowledge and strategies that are essential for improving fitness and maintaining lifelong physical activity

32

Body composition is used to describe the percentages of fat, bone, water, and muscle in bodies. Which of the following is the main concern of body composition as a component of health-related fitness?

A) Muscle formation in the body
B) Relative proportions of fat and lean tissue in the body
C) The relative amount of vitamins present in the body
D) Maintenance of bone mass in the body

33

Norm-referenced tests report whether test takers performed better or worse than a hypothetical average student, which is determined by comparing scores against the performance results of a statistically selected group of test takers, typically of the same age or grade level, who have already taken the exam.

In assessing physical education students, which of the following should be mostly ensured when using standardized, norm-referenced assessment software?

A) The demographic characteristics of the norm group are similar to those of the group being tested.
B) The difficulty of the questions should be level to the lowest performing student.
C) The test should include standardized essay and identification problems.
D) Test items correspond to specific levels of the psychomotor taxonomy.

34

A motor disability is recognized as major when it causes significant and persistent limitations for the person in the course of his or her daily activities. Muscular or neurological systems responsible for body movement are affected, resulting in significant and persistent limitations in a person's daily life.

Which of the following should a teacher do to address a problem on a student with a motor disability who is having difficulty in providing enough force to pass a soccer ball?

A) Assign new lesson for the student
B) Force him to embrace his limitations
C) Transfer the student in other class
D) Shorten the student's length of activity

35

The fitness program is a plan to help someone improve their health and physical condition.

Which of the following sets of health-related components is emphasized in a personal fitness program that performs appropriate stretching exercises during warmup and cool-down for both jogging and weight lifting, jogging 3 days a week for 30–45 minutes and lifting weights 3 days a week?

A) Cardiorespiratory endurance, muscular strength, and flexibility
B) Cardiorespiratory endurance, body composition, and flexibility
C) Cardiorespiratory endurance, muscular strength, and agility
D) Cardiorespiratory endurance, agility, and flexibility

CONTINUE ▶

36

After every vigorous physical activity, cooling-down is performed.

Which of the following is not an immediate physiological benefit of cool-down?

A) Cooldown promotes the reduction of cholesterol in the blood
B) Cooldown prevents blood from pooling in the legs
C) Cooldown reduces the risk of cardiac irregularities
D) Cooldown increases the rate of lactic acid removal from the blood and skeletal muscle

37

Muscular strength is the ability of a person to exert a force on physical objects using muscles. For the development of strength in arms, which of the following sets of exercises should be emphasized?

A) Front curls, bench presses, and shoulder shrugs
B) Front curls, bench presses, and tricep extensions
C) Front curls, overhead presses, and shoulder shrugs
D) Front curls, overhead presses, and tricep extensions

38

The linear relationship between the physiological factor and oxygen consumption is shown in which of the following lists?

A) Red blood cell count, blood type, respiration rate
B) Work rate, heart rate, cardiac rate
C) Blood pressure, work rate, minute ventilation
D) Pulse rate, red blood cell count, core temperature

CONTINUE ▶

39

Sidearm is a motion for throwing a ball along a low, approximately horizontal axis rather than a high, mostly vertical axis (overhand). A baseball coach is teaching his students on the most important element in doing a two-handed side-arm strike to bat a ball.

Which of the following would be his most appropriate cues?

A) "Keep your bat near the ground and create 90-degree angle when the ball is thrown."
B) "Keep your batting elbow flexed during the entire swing and stop the follow-through at the point of contact."
C) "Hold the bat above your shoulder and quickly transfer your body weight sidewards."
D) "Transfer your weight from your back foot to your front foot as your hips and shoulder rotate into the swing."

40

Cardiopulmonary resuscitation (CPR) is a lifesaving technique useful in many emergencies, including heart attack or near drowning.

Which of the following is the main purpose of rescue breathing and chest compressions in doing CPR?

A) Produce electric shock to retrieve heart rhythm
B) Remove any object trapped inside the heart
C) Provide artificial ventilation for a victim who is in severe respiratory distress
D) Oxygenate and circulate the blood in a victim whose heart has stopped beating

CONTINUE ▶

SECTION 2

#	Answer	Topic	Subtopic	#	Answer	Topic	Subtopic	#	Answer	Topic	Subtopic	#	Answer	Topic	Subtopic
1	B	TB	SB1	11	D	TA	SA1	21	B	TA	SA2	31	D	TB	SB2
2	D	TB	SB2	12	C	TB	SB2	22	B	TA	SA1	32	B	TA	SA1
3	B	TB	SB2	13	A	TB	SB3	23	D	TB	SB1	33	A	TB	SB2
4	C	TB	SB1	14	A	TA	SA1	24	D	TB	SB3	34	D	TB	SB3
5	A	TA	SA1	15	D	TA	SA1	25	D	TB	SB2	35	A	TA	SA2
6	C	TB	SB1	16	C	TB	SB3	26	A	TB	SB1	36	A	TA	SA1
7	C	TA	SA2	17	D	TA	SA2	27	B	TB	SB1	37	D	TB	SB3
8	A	TA	SA1	18	A	TA	SA1	28	B	TB	SB1	38	D	TA	SA1
9	B	TB	SB2	19	A	TB	SB2	29	D	TA	SA2	39	D	TB	SB3
10	A	TA	SA2	20	D	TB	SB2	30	B	TB	SB3	40	D	TA	SA1

Topics & Subtopics

Code	Description
SA1	Health Knowledge
SA2	Health Instruction
SB1	Planning Instruction
SB2	Student Growth & Development

Code	Description
SB3	Planning Activities
TA	Health Education
TB	Physical Education

TEST DIRECTION

DIRECTIONS

Read the questions carefully and then choose the ONE best answer to each question.

Be sure to allocate your time carefully so you are able to complete the entire test within the testing session. You may go back and review your answers at any time.

You may use any available space in your test booklet for scratch work.

Questions in this booklet are not actual test questions but they are the samples for commonly asked questions.

This test aims to cover all topics which may appear on the actual test. However some topics may not be covered.

Studying this booklet will be preparing you for the actual test. It will not guarantee improving your test score but it will help you pass your exam on the first attempt.

Some useful tips for answering multiple choice questions;

- Start with the questions that you can easily answer.

- Underline the keywords in the question.

- Be sure to read all the choices given.

- Watch for keywords such as NOT, always, only, all, never, completely.

- Do not forget to answer every question.

1

Before transferring the weight to the other foot, each foot must complete two tasks. This routine is illustrated by which of the following locomotor skills?

A) Side-sliding
B) Jumping
C) Weight lifting
D) Skipping

2

Weight-bearing is the physical state of supporting an applied load while strength training is a type of physical exercise specializing in the use of resistance to induce muscular contraction which builds the strength, anaerobic endurance, and size of skeletal muscles.

Which of the following is the benefit of weight-bearing and strength training exercises to older adults?

A) Reduce the risk of fractures
B) Reduce the risk of coronary diseases
C) Increase respiration rate
D) Increase toned muscles

3

What amount of calories is required to have a negative energy balance in order to lose one pound per week?

A) 3,500
B) 2,500
C) 2,000
D) 1,500

4

Sports is primarily considered as what type of activity as described by most sports sociologists?

A) Generalized
B) Professionalized
C) Idealized
D) Institutionalized

5

The ball is a solid or hollow sphere or ovoid, especially one that is kicked, thrown, or hit in a game.

Which of the following types of the ball should a teacher use to improve catching skills of preschool students who are struggling to catch an 8.5-inch playground ball?

A) Foam ball
B) Basketball
C) Tennis ball
D) Golf ball

6

Target games are activities in which players send an object toward a target while avoiding any obstacles.

Which of the following sports is the best example of a target game?

A) Bocce
B) Badminton
C) Basketball
D) Lacrosse

7

Weight training is a common type of strength training for developing the strength and size of skeletal muscles. To assure safety, which of the following pieces of weight training equipment is most important?

A) Bar collars
B) Dipping Bars
C) Foam roller
D) Rubber cushions

8

Which of the following background influenced the direction of physical education in the late 1800's?

A) Medicine
B) Religion
C) Music
D) Cultural sports

9

Activities in which players send an object toward an object while avoiding any obstacles are called target game.

A target game is best illustrated by which of the following games?

A) Racing
B) Fencing
C) Bocce
D) Indoor court game

10

Which of the following websites provides practical information to individuals, health professionals, nutrition educators, and the food industry to help consumers build healthier diets with resources and tools for dietary assessment, nutrition education, and other user-friendly nutrition information?

A) Nourished Kitchen
B) USDA ChooseMyPlate
C) Calorie Lab
D) Consumer Reports: Health

11

Cooperative games emphasize play rather than the competition while team sport is an activity in which individuals are organized into opposing teams which compete to win.

Which of the following is the contribution of the recreational group and team games such as volleyball in providing social benefits?

A) Pushing all players to their maximum capabilities to uplift the team
B) Promote enjoyment and camaraderie among participants with similar interests
C) Encourage team competition to keep winning the game
D) Keep participants of all fitness levels equally challenged

12

Static balance refers to the ability of a person to maintain the body in some fixed posture. It is also described as the ability of a person to maintain equilibrium.

Which of the following actions demonstrates static balance?

A) Maintaining a handstand position
B) Placing three limbs inside an exercise ring for 5 seconds
C) Standing in place on a balance beam
D) All of the above

13

Acquiring motor skills is just one part of children's development. Mastering both fine and gross motor skills are essential for children's growth and independence. Having good motor control helps children explore the world around them and also helps with their cognitive development.

Which of the following is the most challenging skill to master for children undergoing motor skill development?

A) Catching
B) Galloping
C) Throwing
D) Skipping

14

Which of the following individual had the greatest influence on the direction of physical education in the late 1800s?

A) An individual with a background in professional sport
B) An individual with a background in nutrition
C) An individual with a background in medicine
D) An individual with a background in the intercollegiate sport

15

Aerobic exercises are any of various sustained exercises such as jogging, rowing, swimming, or cycling that stimulate and strengthen the heart and lungs.

By doing regular aerobic exercises, which of the following is the best physiological adaptation in the body?

A) The maximum heartbeat increases
B) The heart can pump more blood throughout the body
C) The lungs are being filtered out of toxins to improve breathing
D) The body is better able to produce energy from fat stored as triglycerides

16

Being a natural leader and positive role model is vital in sports and physical education activities. He should know how to radiate passion with his team members.

Which of the following is needed to be an effective natural leader and positive role mode?

A) Ability to direct members on their wrongdoings
B) Ability to influence a group toward a particular goal in a nonjudgmental, collaborative way
C) Be able to intervene when a problem arises and give disciplinary measures
D) Ability to talk others into a particular course of action in an intentional way

17

Which of the following actions best represents authentic assessment for a basketball skills unit?

A) Making a rubric to evaluate learners as they proceed through the unit
B) Using standardized instruments on basketball skills at the end of the unit
C) Keeping track of the number of baskets made in a class game
D) Using district-devised assessment of skills at the end of the game

18

The school conducted a parent/guardian meeting about the performance of physical education students.

Which of the following is the most important point of discussion?

A) Emphasizing that activities are all student-friendly
B) Doing surveys on the insights of the parent/guardian in their children's progress
C) Describing in detail the assessment tools and techniques used to evaluate student performance
D) Addressing student strengths and achievements in addition to areas needing improvement

19

Which of the following should a teacher initially provide in teaching a closed skill such as a free throw in basketball?

A) A varying rates of skill performance in a varying environment
B) A stable rate of skill performance in a stable environment
C) A varying rates of skill performance in a stable environment
D) A stable rate of skill performance in a varying environment

20

Hopping is to move with light bounding skips or leaps. Which of the following would best explain that hopping will be more appropriate than patterns in introducing students to the rhythmic use of locomotor skills?

A) Controlled movement
B) Requires minimal effort
C) Involves one count and skipping involves two counts.
D) Moves in a different direction as compared to skipping

21

Muscle tone is the continuous and passive partial contraction of the muscles or the muscle's resistance to passive stretch during resting state.

One of your trainees wants to improve overall muscle tone and definition. Which of the following types of fitness training would you recommend?

A) Single weights with decreasing number of repetitions
B) Stretching with holding exercises that muscles hold weights for a minute and gradually increasing
C) Dynamic stretching involving sports movements in which reach, force, and speed are gradually increased
D) Strength training with a moderate degree of resistance and a high number of repetitions

22

Which of the following action should not be considered by a player when dribbling a soccer ball in a restricted space?

A) The player should stay in a slightly crouched position
B) The player should use body feints and changes of speed
C) The player should use only the dominant foot for better control
D) The player should keep the ball close to the feet

23

Educational standards are the learning goals for what students should know and be able to do at each grade level.

Which of the following will be the most probable result in a program by using national and state standards to guide the active development of a curriculum?

A) Control the number of enrolled students to maximize learning.
B) Reflect continuity and coherence across the K–12 scopes.
C) Show the level of competence in each student.
D) Assess student's knowledge before going to college.

24

Throwing is the launching of a ballistic projectile by hand. Which of the following should a physical education teacher do to improve the throwing skill of his students since most of them could not manage to use mature throwing pattern and throw the ball in 30 yards?

A) Prepare activities that highlight speed in throwing the ball.
B) Conduct lessons that emphasize throwing with varied effort.
C) Engage with his students with other classes.
D) Let them observe students with good throwing skills.

25

Which of the following organizations promote and support leadership, research, education, and best practices in the professions that support creative, healthy, and active lifestyles that would be an avenue for physical education teachers to introduce their programs in more population?

A) Department of Education
B) Trail Association
C) Professional Accomplished Practices
D) Society of Health and Physical Educators

26

Motor learning is when complex processes in the brain occur in response to practice or experience of a certain skill resulting in changes in the central nervous system that allows for the production of a new motor skill.

Which of the following stages of motor learning does the student is concerned with performing and refining the skills?

A) Associative stage
B) Dissociative stage
C) Autonomous stage
D) Cognitive stage

27

The study shows strong and consistent evidence from observational studies that physical inactivity and poor fitness are associated with higher illness and death from all causes.

Which of the following diseases occurs mostly in people with poor fitness level and inactivity to physical activities?

A) Migraines
B) Fever and allergies
C) High blood pressure
D) Bacterial infection

28

The progressive overload principle basically states: In order for a muscle to grow, strength to be gained, performance to increase, or for any similar improvement to occur, the human body must be forced to adapt to a tension that is above and beyond what it has previously experienced.

An athlete is designing a variable-resistance training program to develop muscular endurance rather than strength. Which of the following best describes the application of the principle of progressive overload?

A) Gradually increasing the number of repetitions of resistance exercises
B) Increasing the duration of rest intervals on one exercise over time
C) Decreasing the training time for each exercise
D) Increasing the weight that the muscles can hold

29

In physical education class, the maximum heart rate that should characterize students' exercise for health-related fitness is best expressed by which of the following heart rate percentage?

A) A maximum heart rate of 10-35%
B) A maximum heart rate of 35-60%
C) A maximum heart rate of 60-85%
D) A maximum heart rate of 85-95%

30

Cross-training refers to combining exercises of other disciplines, different than that of the athlete in training. Swimming and jogging could be an example of cross-training activities.

Which of the following is the best physiological change in the body after weeks of doing cross-training activities?

A) Increased weight of muscles
B) Improved bone mass and strength
C) Improved ratio of high-density lipoproteins (HDLs) to low-density lipoproteins (LDLs)
D) Increased length of long bones and decreased length of tendons attached to long bones

31

Breaststroke is a swimming technique in which the swimmer's face is in the water and the arms move in a large motion from front to back as the feet kick outward.

Which of the following are the two common mistakes demonstrated by novice swimmers who are just learning the breaststroke?

A) Moving the arms too fast; Carrying the arms too high in the recovery
B) Pulling the arms back too far; Improper timing between movements of the legs and the arms
C) Moving the arms too fast; Pulling the arms back too far
D) Failure to relax; Improper timing between movements of the legs and the arms

32

An implement is a piece of equipment, primarily used for a particular purpose.

What is the direct relationship of the difficulty of striking a ball with a tool like a tennis racket, a bat, or golf club?

A) The difficulty of striking a ball decreases with the length of the implement.
B) The difficulty of striking a ball increases with the length of the implement.
C) The difficulty of striking a ball stays the same with the length of the implement.
D) No direct relationship on the difficulty of striking a ball with an implement.

33

Bernard Weiner, American social psychologist, created the attribution theory of motivation as a framework to explain why people do what they do. He stated that people seek causal factors that allow them to maintain a positive self-image, and it is these attributions that determine an individual's motivation to repeat behaviors.

Which of the following should the students be based on teachers' preference in the attribution motivational theory?

A) Be motivated by external rewards.
B) Be motivated by interest or enjoyment without relying on external rewards.
C) Attribute their successes and failures to factors within their own control.
D) Attribute their successes and failures to factors outside their own control.

34

In order to set appropriate health-related goals, which of the following assessment techniques will most likely help students?

A) Complete a fitness tests
B) Compute every calorie intake
C) Keep track of other students improvement on weight training
D) Reading journals, books, and essays about sports and sport rules

35

Field hockey is an outdoor game played on a grass field between two teams of 11 players who use long curved sticks to hit a small ball and try to score goals while indoor floor hockey is usually in the style of ice hockey, that are played on flat floor surfaces, such as a basketball court.

Which of the following would be the basic rule of field hockey and indoor floor hockey?

A) Excessive body contact or stick-to-stick contact is not allowed.
B) Players must elevate the stick above chest level when doing follow-through.
C) Players must hold the stick, on the one hand, all the time.
D) Players can hold the ball before going out of the line.

36

When will the maximum force be exerted on the ball at impact when swinging a tennis racket?

A) The speed of the strike should remain constant before impact with the ball.
B) The player should minimize extending his shoulder muscles as preparation for backswing.
C) The angular velocity of the swinging implement should be constant throughout.
D) The angular velocity of the swinging implement is as fast as possible.

37

Developmental psychology is concerned with the scientific understanding of age-related changes in experience and behavior, not only in children but throughout the lifespan.

Which of the following best explains the role of playing in young children's growth and development according to principles of developmental psychology?

A) Play allows children to observe other children's behavior towards others
B) Play allows children to try out and test new physical, cognitive, and social behaviors, which then become part of their working memory
C) Play allows children to understand the environment and issues to be taken
D) Play provides important information about gender roles, children with limited opportunities to play often experience delayed development of gender identity

38

Adolescence typically describes the years between ages 13 and 19. It can be considered the transitional stage from childhood to adulthood. However, it can start earlier, during the preteen or "tween" years.

In the adolescent stage of human growth and development, which of the following cognitive mile-stones can be best associated?

A) Having short attention span and easily distracted
B) Learning to take intentions into account in judging the behaviors of others
C) Readiness to conform to the spoken word
D) Building interest in abstract ideas and the process of thinking itself

39

Dribbling in soccer is the way in which soccer players advance the ball with their feet. A soccer coach is trying to emphasize players on points when dribbling a soccer ball.

Which of the following is the most appropriate technique?

A) Keeping the ball in straight motion without going out in any direction
B) Using a running motion to travel and delivering a series of taps to the ball with the foot
C) Keeping eye on the direction of the motion of the ball
D) Moving at a speed faster than a walk and keeping the ball within two to four feet of the body

40

Negligence is a term that means carelessness or a breach of an obligation. In case of a student acquiring injury in a physical education class, which of the following teaching practices will protect the teacher from possible charges of negligence?

A) Doing group feedback discussions than individual evaluation
B) Allowing students not to participate in activities they are not fine doing
C) Providing students with developmentally-appropriate instruction based on recommended skills progressions
D) Ensuring that the students always have a written copy of instructions

SECTION 3

#	Answer	Topic	Subtopic
1	D	TB	SB1
2	A	TB	SB2
3	A	TB	SB3
4	D	TB	SB3
5	A	TB	SB3
6	A	TB	SB3
7	A	TB	SB3
8	A	TB	SB3
9	C	TB	SB1
10	B	TA	SA2

#	Answer	Topic	Subtopic
11	B	TB	SB2
12	D	TB	SB3
13	D	TB	SB2
14	C	TB	SB2
15	D	TA	SA1
16	B	TB	SB1
17	A	TB	SB1
18	D	TB	SB2
19	B	TB	SB1
20	C	TB	SB3

#	Answer	Topic	Subtopic
21	D	TB	SB2
22	C	TB	SB3
23	B	TB	SB1
24	B	TB	SB3
25	D	TB	SB3
26	A	TB	SB2
27	C	TA	SA1
28	A	TB	SB2
29	C	TA	SA2
30	C	TA	SA1

#	Answer	Topic	Subtopic
31	B	TB	SB3
32	B	TB	SB3
33	C	TB	SB1
34	A	TB	SB2
35	A	TB	SB3
36	D	TB	SB3
37	B	TB	SB2
38	D	TB	SB2
39	B	TB	SB3
40	C	TA	SA2

Topics & Subtopics

Code	Description
SA1	Health Knowledge
SA2	Health Instruction
SB1	Planning Instruction
SB2	Student Growth & Development

Code	Description
SB3	Planning Activities
TA	Health Education
TB	Physical Education

TEST DIRECTION

DIRECTIONS

Read the questions carefully and then choose the ONE best answer to each question.

Be sure to allocate your time carefully so you are able to complete the entire test within the testing session. You may go back and review your answers at any time.

You may use any available space in your test booklet for scratch work.

Questions in this booklet are not actual test questions but they are the samples for commonly asked questions.

This test aims to cover all topics which may appear on the actual test. However some topics may not be covered.

Studying this booklet will be preparing you for the actual test. It will not guarantee improving your test score but it will help you pass your exam on the first attempt.

Some useful tips for answering multiple choice questions;

- Start with the questions that you can easily answer.

- Underline the keywords in the question.

- Be sure to read all the choices given.

- Watch for keywords such as NOT, always, only, all, never, completely.

- Do not forget to answer every question.

1

Which of the following would be the most appropriate ruling when two opposing players hit the volleyball net at the same time?

A) Sideout
B) Replay
C) Substitution
D) No gain/loss point

2

In the given choices, which activity is the most aerobically demanding in terms of kcal/hour burned?

A) Volleyball
B) Walking
C) Cross-country skiing
D) Bowling

3

Bowling refers to a series of sports or leisure activities in which a player rolls or throws a bowling ball towards a target.

Which of the following basic bowling skills should be reviewed first before practicing?

A) Retrieving the bowling ball
B) Proper stance
C) Choosing a grip that is comfortable
D) Tallying scores

4

Badminton is a racquet sport played using racquets to hit a shuttlecock across a net. In badminton, which of the following would be the most critical element on a ready position?

A) Holding the racket up
B) Holding the racket sidewards
C) Bending knees
D) Putting feet together

5. Which of the following exercises consists of low-impact flexibility and muscular strength and endurance movements which emphasize proper postural alignment, core strength, and muscle balance?

A) Inline skating
B) Aerobics
C) Pilates
D) Cross-country skiing

6. The beat is defined as a rhythmic movement or is the speed at which a piece of music is played.

Which of the following is musical note played by a music student when he claps in each beat twice in an even rhythm of eight-beat measure?

A) Eighth notes
B) Sixteenth notes
C) Quarter notes
D) Downbeats

7. Which of the following concept is promoted by throwing a ball back and forth against your partner with increasing distance?

A) Range
B) Accuracy
C) Precision
D) Speed

8. Development is defined as the process of growth.

Which of the following type of development is exhibited by a student who enjoys doing physical activities and achieves a feeling of satisfaction?

A) Merit
B) Cognitive
C) Affective
D) Coordination

9

A weekend athlete who exercises vigorously only on weekends, but not regularly during the week, does not exercise often enough to see solid results.

Which of the following principles of training does he violate?

A) The principle of progression
B) The principle of rest and recovery
C) The principle of reversibility
D) The principle of specificity of exercise

10

Formative assessment refers to a wide variety of methods that teachers use to conduct in-process evaluations.

Which of the following is the main advantage formative assessment strategies?

A) Provide teachers the comparison for student's individual and group learning.
B) Provide a copy of the basis of evaluation of parents to the learning of their children.
C) Provide both teachers and students with invaluable information about what students understand, and what they don't.
D) Provide standardized data that captures the degree to which students have achieved learning outcomes.

11

Ms. Dianne, a physical education teacher, asks her students to keep a journal about how they felt about each activity during a physical education unit focusing on the development of health-related fitness.

What is the purpose of the activity of keeping a journal?

A) For differentiated instruction
B) For identification and recall of information
C) For standards-based instruction
D) For criterion-referenced grading

12

Self-confidence is how you feel about your abilities and can vary from situation to situation while self-esteem reflects a person's overall subjective emotional evaluation of his or her own worth.

Which of the following type of benefit is gained from regular exercise when there is an increase in self-confidence and self-esteem through one's improvement of appearance and ability to perform tasks?

A) Psychological
B) Cognitive
C) Free-spirited
D) Physical

13

Quality of movement is moving from the inside out, initiating with the breath while maintaining oppositional energy and active engagement from the fingertips to the toes.

Which of the following activities would be most effective in demonstrating the effort quality of movement?

A) Making different shapes while hanging from a bar
B) Dribbling basketball between cones
C) Throwing volleyball upwards continuously
D) Touching bars in different heights

14

Plyometrics is an exercise involving repeated rapid stretching and contracting of muscles, like in jumping and rebounding, to increase muscle power.

Which of the following is the purpose of plyometrics?

A) It is appropriate for explosive power training.
B) It is used to improved flexibility.
C) It is used for muscular endurance.
D) It is used for cardiovascular fitness.

15

Hereditary is a descriptive term for conditions capable of being transmitted from parent to offspring through the genes.

Which of the following areas of personal growth and development is the general contribution of hereditary involve?

A) Character quality towards building relationships
B) Development of diseases acquired from stress
C) Body type and composition
D) Level of physical strength towards training

16

A cross-curricular approach to teaching is characterized by sensitivity towards, and synthesis of, knowledge, skills, and understandings from various subject areas.

Which of the following is the benefit of cross-curricular links to physical education students?

A) Increase in respect of students to teachers
B) Increase in the students' time in class
C) Increase awareness by students of the relevance of all subjects
D) Increase number of lessons learned

17

Which of the following is not a significant component of the Whole School, Whole Community, Whole Child (WSCC) model?

A) Employee wellness
B) Health insurance for students
C) Community involvement
D) Comprehensive school health education

18

Muscle strength is the ability to exert a maximal amount of force for a short period of time while endurance training is the act of exercising to increase endurance.

Which of the following is the result of muscular strength and endurance training in the composition of the body?

A) Muscle mass increases with possible fat reduction
B) Muscle is enlarged due to fat accumulation
C) There is a high loss of weight due to fat elimination
D) Muscles atrophy as fat is reduced

19

The most commonly known throw in disc golf is the backhand. It derives its name from tennis because the motion (having the arms cross over in front of the body, then moving outward and releasing with the arm extended before the body) is reminiscent of the tennis stroke.

Which of the following is being achieved when the back of the hand is kept parallel with the ground during a backhand disc throw, and the release is flat rather than at an angle?

A) Making the disc fly farther
B) Giving a slight backward movement after the flight
C) Forming an S-shaped pathway
D) Flying the disc diagonally to hit the ground

20

"Simon Says" is a child's game for 3 or more players where 1 player takes the role of "Simon" and issues instructions (usually physical actions such as "jump in the air" or "stick out your tongue") to the other players which should only be followed if prefaced with the phrase "Simon says".

Which of the following is the purpose of the game "Simon Says" in evaluating kindergarten students' ability?

A) Develop balance and strength
B) Develop teamwork and coordination skills
C) Distinguish among locomotor skills
D) Demonstrate body awareness concepts

21

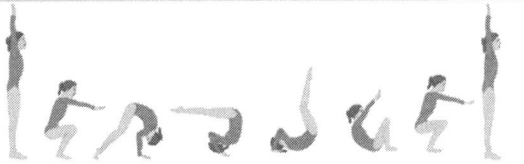

Forward roll also called as roly-poly is one of the essential elements in gymnastics.

Which of the following is the most commonly encountered problem in doing the forward roll considering the primitive stage of the action?

A) Losing the curl
B) Keeping the chin tucked
C) Keeping hips and knees flexed
D) Using the hands to cushion the head contact

22

A curriculum model determines the type of curriculum used; it encompasses educational philosophy, approach to teaching, and methodology.

A physical education class activity for the 5th-grade student is done by the pair. One student finds out how his pair is making mistakes. Students switch roles on the teacher's signal.

Which of the following is the curriculum model used by the teacher?

A) Problem-solving model
B) Eclectic approaches
C) Cooperative Learning Model
D) Peer Teaching Model

23

Stewardship is an ethic that embodies the responsible planning and management of resources.

Which of the following will develop stewardship of students toward the environment in an outdoor education program?

A) Reminding students to bring fewer things for a day out
B) Teaching students on the major viewpoints of the place
C) Requiring students to participate in environmental campaigns
D) Teaching students Leave No Trace principles and how to apply them in any outdoor setting

24

Milo was a six-time wrestling champion at the Ancient Olympic Games in Greece. It is believed that Milo lifted a newborn bull onto his shoulders each day until the bull became fully mature.

Which two principles of modern muscle strength and endurance conditioning did Milo follow?

A) Progression and Frequency
B) Retention and Intensity
C) Overload and Variable resistance
D) Overload and Progression

25

A toddler is a child 12 to 36 months old. The toddler years are a time of great cognitive, emotional and social development. The word is derived from "to toddle," which means to hobble, like a child of this age.

Which of the following is the main reason that toddlers learn to run after several months of learning to walk?

A) Running requires softer muscles which develop later on a toddler.
B) Running involves supporting body weight in all phases and thus requires additional strength.
C) Running is more stable and requires higher body mass.
D) Running is less stable and requires the development of greater motor control and coordination.

26

A blister is a painful swelling on the skin, often filled with a watery liquid, caused by a burn or by rubbing against something.

Which of the following precautions should be taken into consideration to prevent blisters in hiking?

A) Keeping hydrated before hiking
B) Warming up on cold days of hiking
C) Wearing socks that air cannot damp onto the skin
D) Wearing sturdy, proper-fitting hiking shoes that have been broken in

27

A student was so frustrated since he does not get the gold medal in the swimming competition. His coach told him that he was so sorry to see him disappointed besides doing all the training.

Why is the coach's response appropriate?

A) It provides an objective overview.
B) It affirms that the student set a goal and worked hard.
C) It shows appreciation for the student's performance.
D) It emphasizes the coach's knowledge of his student's span of practice.

28

Fitness plan includes exercises to help someone improve their health and physical condition.

Which of the following is an initial consideration in making activities for a personal fitness plan?

A) Choosing activities that are less costly and easy to execute
B) Researching other group exercise activities which one can be involved
C) Determining the type of physical activities that one enjoys
D) Considering which types of activities are weather dependent and which are available year-round

29

Adolescence is the period of developmental transition between childhood and adulthood, involving multiple physical, intellectual, personality, and social developmental changes.

In the physical growth of infants and toddlers, which of the following is the typical development?

A) Physical growth occurs first in the head and proceeds downward to the trunk and outward toward the extremities.
B) Physical growth occurs in sudden changes in body shape and height.
C) Physical growth occurs variably in individuals with no typical starting point or progression of growth.
D) Physical growth co-occurs throughout the body.

30

The belayer is the person on the ground who secures the climber, keeping a close eye on the climber's progress and letting out slack to the line by releasing the belay.

In indoor rock climbing, which of the following should a belayer do to make sure the safety of a climber?

A) Keeping the brake hand in the "lock off" position when there is no slack or movement by the climber
B) Reminding the climber to hold closer to the edge
C) Instructing the climber where and when to take a step
D) Maintaining a secure position beneath the climber and as close to the wall as possible.

31

Stability is the ability of a substance to remain unchanged over time. People with large body builds tend to excel at physical activities that require a great degree of stability.

Which of the following could be the best explanation?

A) Size of the body is directly proportional to the force exerted.
B) People with large body have faster movement than people with smaller body segments.
C) Muscles with large cross-sectional areas can produce more force than smaller muscles.
D) A body's inertia, or resistance to change in a state of motion, is proportional to body mass.

32

Physical fitness is a state of health and well-being and, more specifically, the ability to perform aspects of sports, occupations and daily activities. Physical fitness is generally achieved through proper nutrition, moderate-vigorous physical exercise, and sufficient rest.

Which of the following would be the most appropriate action to develop a cognitive lesson that includes health-enhancing physical fitness to 8th-grade students?

A) Instruct students to have a one-mile fitness assessment with a heart rate monitor
B) Instruct students to create a webpage demonstrating an understanding of the fitness components.
C) Instruct students to assess their fitness levels with a help of a parent or guardian
D) Instruct students to survey each other's level of physical fitness

33

The underhand throw is performed with the hand below the level of the elbow or the arm below the level of the shoulder. A teacher is teaching children to throw a ball using an underhand throw.

Which of the following is the most appropriate technique?

A) Bring dominant hand back until the height of elbow is equal to the height of shoulder while facing dominant arm upward at a 90-degree angle.

B) Holding the ball with both hands at your chest with both fingers spread around the ball

C) Taking one step forward with the foot opposite the throwing hand

D) Positioning both feet on the ground, taking the ball in both hands back and over the head, and without breaking your momentum, releasing the ball with both hands

34

Building bigger and stronger biceps have always been desired by men throughout the world. The standing barbell curl is an effective isolation exercise that works your bicep muscles, along with training the muscles in the shoulders and the forearms.

Which of the following best describes the generation of force during a standing barbell curl by a muscle group?

A) The generation of force varies throughout the full range of motion.

B) The generation of force remains constant throughout the full range of motion.

C) The maximal force-development capacity should remain constant as the weight is lifted above waist-level.

D) There should be no maximal force-development as the weight is lifted above waist-level.

35

Heat exhaustion is a condition whose symptoms may include heavy sweating and a rapid pulse, a result of your body overheating. A student suddenly fell to the ground while playing outdoor fun games activities. As an initial response, the teacher moved the student into a shady area and check signs of heat exhaustion.

Which of the following should be the teacher's next step?

A) Call the ambulance and do not move the student
B) Give the student sips of water or a sports drink
C) Sprinkle water on student's face
D) Cover the student with a light blanket and elevate his or feet

36

Strength training is a type of physical exercise specializing in the use of resistance to induce muscular contraction which builds the strength, anaerobic endurance, and size of skeletal muscles.

Which of the following should be the trainer's response to a female student that wants to do strength-training exercises without developing large muscles?

A) Training promotes considerable gains in strength but only slight increases in muscle bulk because of females' low testosterone levels.
B) Training develops large muscles on lower extremities for females due to shorter built.
C) Training has a minimal effect on muscle strength for females since females tend to develop stronger bones.
D) Toned muscles are necessary for gains in size and strength, so only females who begin training with well-defined muscles will develop larger ones.

37

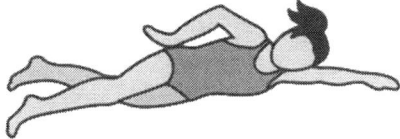

A crawl is a swimming stroke in which arms are moved alternately overhead accompanied by a flutter kick.

Which of the following is the main reason that crawl is defined as continuous or repetitive motor tasks?

A) Recovery of the arms and legs leads directly into the next stroke, with no recognizable beginning and end
B) A variation of the front crawl where one arm always rests at the front while the other arm performs one cycle
C) Arms stay in the water and move synchronously, while the legs perform a whip kick
D) Movement through the water can be sustained with no physical effort by keeping the body flat in the water

38

An open motor skill is a skill which is performed in an unstable environment where the start point is determined by the environment.

Which of the following describes an open motor skill?

A) The participant often performs the skill in an unpredictable, changing environment
B) The participant often performs the skill in an environment with constant conditions
C) The skill can be performed in precisely the same way each time regardless of the context
D) Open motor skills are typically easier to perform as they involve less variability and complexity of factors to be accounted for

39

Which of the following is the advantage of a school-community collaboration that offers free services on local fitness facility to high school students that have undergone fitness instruction in class?

A) The collaboration allows physical education teachers to reallocate time usually spent on fitness to other instructional areas.
B) Previewing the facility improves chances that students will continue to use it, which benefits both the facility and students.
C) The collaboration allows students to divert from any detrimental factors and acquires less stress.
D) The collaboration allows students to manage their money management.

40

With the help of *cooperative games*, students can become critical thinkers, learn to work with one another, and apply these skills to accomplish team goals.

Which of the following opportunities do cooperative games and team sports provide in developing positive traits and values for students?

A) Test individual's limit and patience.
B) Stay calm even working under pressure.
C) Study and emulate the interpersonal skills of a variety of adult role models.
D) Observe and practice character-building skills such as determination, loyalty, self-control, and civility.

SECTION 4

#	Answer	Topic	Subtopic	#	Answer	Topic	Subtopic	#	Answer	Topic	Subtopic	#	Answer	Topic	Subtopic
1	B	TB	S3	11	A	TB	S1	21	A	TB	S3	31	D	TB	S3
2	C	TB	S3	12	A	TB	S2	22	D	TB	S1	32	B	TB	S2
3	C	TB	S3	13	A	TB	S3	23	D	TB	S3	33	C	TB	S3
4	A	TB	S3	14	A	TB	S3	24	D	TB	S2	34	A	TB	S3
5	C	TB	S3	15	C	TB	S2	25	D	TB	S2	35	B	TB	S1
6	B	TB	S3	16	C	TB	S1	26	D	TB	S3	36	A	TB	S2
7	A	TB	S1	17	B	TB	S3	27	B	TB	S3	37	A	TB	S3
8	C	TB	S2	18	A	TB	S2	28	C	TB	S1	38	A	TB	S2
9	A	TB	S3	19	A	TB	S3	29	A	TB	S2	39	B	TB	S2
10	C	TB	S1	20	D	TB	S2	30	A	TB	S3	40	D	TB	S2

Topics & Subtopics

Code	Description	Code	Description
SB1	Planning Instruction	SB3	Planning Activities
SB2	Student Growth & Development	TB	Physical Education

CONTINUE ▶

TEST DIRECTION

DIRECTIONS

Read the questions carefully and then choose the ONE best answer to each question.

Be sure to allocate your time carefully so you are able to complete the entire test within the testing session. You may go back and review your answers at any time.

You may use any available space in your test booklet for scratch work.

Questions in this booklet are not actual test questions but they are the samples for commonly asked questions.

This test aims to cover all topics which may appear on the actual test. However some topics may not be covered.

Studying this booklet will be preparing you for the actual test. It will not guarantee improving your test score but it will help you pass your exam on the first attempt.

Some useful tips for answering multiple choice questions;

- Start with the questions that you can easily answer.

- Underline the keywords in the question.

- Be sure to read all the choices given.

- Watch for keywords such as NOT, always, only, all, never, completely.

- Do not forget to answer every question.

1

Which of the following skills is the reason why the activity patterns of a five-year-old child are more physically demanding than younger children?

A) Cognitive skills
B) Gross-motor skills
C) Social skills
D) Manipulative skills

2

A physical education teacher wants to have several lessons at a time. He wants students to move from one station to the next, within a specific time frame, to engage in all activities.

Which of the following teaching strategies should he use?

A) Parallel teaching
B) Team teaching
C) Cooperative teaching
D) Station teaching

3

Weightlifting is the activity of lifting heavy objects for exercise. Which of the following weightlifting exercises should the physical education teacher suggest to an offensive lineman on the football team who wants to increase his chest power for blocking?

A) Goblet squat
B) Pallof press
C) Bench press
D) Deadlift

4

Which of the following areas of development is addressed when a grade school teacher creates a program that develops students' appreciation and enjoyment in the group and also promotes the sense of self-worth?

A) Communication development
B) Movement skills
C) Social-emotional development
D) Moral development

5. Which of the following exercises would promote core strength and endurance which is essential in back support and core stability?

A) Plank
B) Abdominal curl-up
C) Bicycle crunch
D) One arm toe touch crunch

6. Body composition is used to describe the percentages of fat, bone, water, and muscle in human bodies. To measure body composition, which of the following instruments would give the most accurate results?

A) Skin calipers
B) Tape measure
C) Balanced scale
D) T-ray detectors

7. Knowing workout and exercise goal is a critical step in creating the best workout routine. To help a student establish individual fitness goals, which of the following should be a teacher's initial step?

A) Evaluate student's pre-fitness test.
B) Assess the student's health-related fitness levels.
C) Survey his/her family about the student's physical activity levels.
D) Watch the student performs fitness test.

8. Task cards are a set of cards that have tasks or questions written on them. When teaching physical education skills, which of the following is the main advantage of using commercially-prepared task cards?

A) Students can refer to the cards as needed for written cues and visual images of proper techniques.
B) Information on cards can easily be changed in case of corrections to the lessons.
C) Evaluation of the students' performance can be tracked and managed faster.
D) Teachers can be assured that students will demonstrate consistency in performing skills.

9

An opportunity to reflect on what should students learn and they need to improve is best allowed by which of the following instructional models?

A) Cooperative learning
B) Self-reviewing
C) Group studying
D) Weekly reading and solving problems

10

Why is it essential for the physical education teacher to routinely check the first aid kit, batteries in the defibrillator, holes in the playing fields and other equipment as preparation for class?

A) To support school's vision and mission
B) To assist other staff members to fulfill their duty
C) To create s safe physical education learning environment
D) To implement the school's physical education curriculum

11

How would a wrestler learn a new takedown technique considering the applications of technology?

A) By viewing recordings of his wrestling performances
B) By reading about the proper technique and procedure on the internet
C) By viewing a series of pictures showing proper execution on a video screen
D) By exchanging e-mail messages with other wrestlers about their experience of learning the technique

12

Cognitive thinking refers to the use of mental activities and skills to perform tasks such as learning, reasoning, understanding, remembering and paying attention.

In order to determine a student's cognitive understanding of the mechanics of a particular skill, which of the following methods would be the most effective?

A) Observe the student doing the skill.
B) Listen to the student teach another student the skill.
C) Allow the student to evaluate his skill development.
D) Prepare a pen and paper examination.

13

The practice session is a period of training that takes place over a set period.

Which of the following would be necessary before practice session of a folk-dance unit?

A) Review of the previous practice session
B) Repetition of the difficult steps
C) Individual presentation for future steps reference
D) Exercises and stretches to warm up muscles and joints before working on the routine

14

Muscle contraction is the activation of tension-generating sites within muscle fibers. Which of the following are the means of production of force in an isometric muscle contraction?

A) As a response to extension of joint
B) As a response to a greater opposing movement with elongation
C) Through tension and muscle contraction without movement
D) Through movement generated in opposition to the downward pull of gravity

15

Which of the following will have a bad result in contact sport wherein participants necessarily come into bodily contact with one another?

A) Enlarging field area dimensions
B) Assigning individual roles for each student
C) Forming teams in which one player is bigger, stronger, or more skilled than the other
D) Coaching students with different offensive and defensive styles

16

Which of the following is the purpose of having a correct racing posture when an athlete is a swimmer, a cyclist of a downhill skier?

A) The correct racing posture minimizes the effect of propulsion.
B) The correct racing posture minimizes the effect of lift.
C) The correct racing posture minimizes the effect of gravity.
D) The correct racing posture minimizes the effect of drag.

CONTINUE ▶

17

Equity is the quality of being fair and impartial. In making an appropriate instruction for physical education, which of the following is the most critical core equity issues that the teacher must consider?

A) Values to be developed in sport activities
B) Differences in taking instructions and setting goals
C) Standards to be used and individual knowledge
D) Gender, individual differences in experience and skill level, and cultural relevance

18

The legislation is a law which has been promulgated by a legislature or other governing body or the process of making it.

Which of the following is the leading factor in legislative and policy changes impacting physical education?

A) Increase in childhood obesity
B) Increase in cases of malnutrition
C) Increase in cases of eating disorders
D) Increase in number of students who do not engage in sports

19

Which of the following will result in a flawless run of physical education in elementary?

A) Implement strict rules of no interruptions during class.
B) Prepare the activity space and having the necessary equipment on hand prior to lesson activities.
C) Group students to lessen the load of program instruction.
D) Establish and announce to students time goals for each lesson activity

20

In developing a manual of safety procedures for a physical education program, which of the following should be included?

I. Teachers must mark appropriate traffic patterns around the throwing area in javelin classes.

II. Students must read and sign a copy of the rules for archery classes.

III. Before soccer classes start, teachers must personally inspect playing fields.

IV. During aerobic fitness activities, students must exercise at or below 50% of their maximal heart rate.

A) I and III
B) II and IV
C) I, II and III
D) II, III, and IV

21

Body composition is used to describe the percentages of fat, bone, water and muscle in bodies while body image is person's perception of the aesthetics or sexual attractiveness of their own body.

In order to develop good attitude in children about their body composition and body image, which of the following will be the best approach?

A) Telling children to determine their body mass index and explain its manifestation
B) Teaching children the different diets and eating patterns
C) Emphasizing that individuals come in a variety of sizes and shapes within a range of healthy body weights
D) Instructing children to observe their families' eating habit and adapt them

22

The forward roll is a movement in which one's body is rolled forward, by putting the head on the ground and swinging the legs over the head.

Which of the following would be the most appropriate solution of a teacher when he repeatedly observes that his students' execution of forwarding roll is unsuccessful because one student rolls in a crooked line and bumps into the next student after him?

A) Give the student separate activity to work on
B) Change the position of the student and put him into a larger area
C) Change the activity in which all can execute the act successfully
D) Observe the student's roll to assess movement technique and provide individualized instruction.

23

The Whole School, Whole Community, Whole Child or WSCC model is an expansion and update of the Coordinated School Health approach. This model incorporates the components CSH and the principles of ASCD's (Association for Supervision and Curriculum Development) whole child approach to strengthening a unified and collaborative approach to learning and health.

Which of the following does WSCC model include?

A) Nutrition and environment services
B) Comprehensive school health education
C) Physical education and physical activity
D) All of the above

24

Digital media refers to audio, video, and photo content that has been encoded while word processing is the phrase used to describe using a computer to create, edit, and print documents.

A teacher asks his 7th-grade students to document their assessment of own fitness through digital media and word processing. Which of the following should a teacher suggest to protect the privacy of the students' work?

A) Open their post for public view.
B) Instruct students to gather information through the Internet.
C) Post their project on a secured website for the teacher to review.
D) Share their post in public view and name the author as anonymous.

25

Self-esteem reflects a person's overall subjective emotional evaluation of his or her worth.

Which of the following does outdoor education bring to students in promoting their self-esteem?

A) Having alone time for self-reflection
B) Having time for meditation
C) Experience a sense of accomplishment in reaching a goal or destination.
D) Attempt to set personal best records each time one participates.

26

A code of professional conduct is a necessary component of any profession to maintain standards for the individuals within that profession to adhere. It brings about accountability, responsibility and trust to the individuals that the profession serves.

Based on professional codes of conduct for physical educators, which of the following is an unethical practice?

A) Discuss student's issues with his/her parent/guardian in helping the student.
B) Use a physical education assessment tool or test for a purpose for which it was not designed or validated.
C) Revise instruction based on informal data assessment.
D) Compile group results in suggesting improvement or need of other fitness resources.

27

The adolescent growth spurt is a rapid increase in the individual's height and weight during puberty resulting from the simultaneous release of growth hormones, thyroid hormones, and androgens.

Which of the following is the result of the changes in the proportion of limb-to-torso-length when an adolescent's arms and legs grow longer?

A) Poor tissue elasticity
B) Increase in flexibility and balance
C) Periods of poor coordination and balance
D) Formation of toned and flexible muscles

28

Spatial awareness is the ability to be aware of oneself in space. It is an organized knowledge of objects in relation to oneself in that given space. Spatial awareness also involves understanding the relationship of these objects when there is a change of position.

Which of the following activities should a teacher facilitate for his kindergarten class to learn spatial awareness?

A) Throwing ball upwards
B) Doing group run relay
C) Playing a tag game
D) Balancing on body parts

29

Motor learning is when complex processes in the brain occur in response to practice or experience of a particular skill resulting in changes in the central nervous system that allows for the production of a new motor skill.

A physical education teacher wants to assess his student's progress in mastering a new motor task. Which of the following would be the most effective assessment strategy?

A) Instructing the student to create individual self-assessment
B) Conducting observations of the student's performance of the task in familiar practice or game situation
C) Giving out post-test exam test that involves questions about the motor task
D) Determining whether the student has progressed from the cognitive stage of motor learning to the associative stage

30

A physical education teacher tells the student that he shoots the ball with proper hand position and suggests to bend the student's knees more.

Which of the following is the means of the teacher to improve the performance of the student?

A) Sets another challenge for the student to go beyond his potential.
B) Instruct with simple terms.
C) Combines positive specific feedback with encouragement to correct one component of the skill
D) Define the motor task in visual terms for the student and provides spatial directions.

SECTION 5

#	Answer	Topic	Subtopic
1	B	TB	S2
2	D	TB	S1
3	C	TB	S2
4	C	TB	S2
5	B	TB	S1
6	C	TB	S3
7	B	TB	S1
8	A	TB	S1

#	Answer	Topic	Subtopic
9	A	TB	S1
10	D	TB	S3
11	A	TB	S3
12	B	TB	S2
13	D	TB	S3
14	C	TB	S3
15	C	TB	S3
16	D	TB	S3

#	Answer	Topic	Subtopic
17	D	TB	S2
18	A	TB	S3
19	B	TB	S2
20	C	TB	S3
21	C	TB	S3
22	D	TB	S3
23	D	TB	S3
24	C	TB	S3

#	Answer	Topic	Subtopic
25	C	TB	S2
26	B	TB	S2
27	C	TB	S3
28	D	TB	S2
29	B	TB	S1
30	C	TB	S2

Topics & Subtopics

Code	Description
SB1	Planning Instruction
SB2	Student Growth & Development
SB3	Planning Activities
TB	Physical Education

Made in the USA
Lexington, KY
21 September 2018